Uff Da!
Let's Dance!

Scandinavian Tunes &
House Party Music
for Accordion

MB20974

by Bruce Bollerud

"Uff da" is a mild exclamation used by Norwegian Americans in a variety of surprising, embarassing, or difficult situations. "Uff da" is like "Oh my gosh"! or "oh dear!" You say "uff da" when you back into the boss' car or when your wife whispers at a dinner party, "Ole, you got some lettuce stuck to your front teeth, uff da." You might say "uff da" under your breath as you realize that the "old friend" you are chatting with at the grocery store is not whom you thought he was. You have no idea who this person is and he hasn't a clue who you are, uff da. In this context of this book, "uff da" means something like "Oh well, life is life, let's dance!"

— Bruce Bollerud

Recording produced by Dix Bruce. Music engraving and book by Dix Bruce.
Special thanks to Lorna Joy Swain for her wonderful proofing and suggestions.

Also by Bruce Bollerud: "International Accordion Favorites"
Waltzes, Polkas, Tangos, Hornpipes, Two-Steps, and more!"

Cover illustration © 2009 Elwood H. Smith

Free audio available online!
Visit: www.melbay.com/20974

Visit us on the Web at www.melbay.com or www.billsmusicshelf.com

Contents

CD Contents

Introduction

I was born in 1934, so I caught the end of the House Party era. This music had its hey-day during the depression when people didn't have much money and didn't travel too far from home. There was a homespun charm to the House Party and in remembering those times I've often heard old timers say "We didn't have much money so we made our own fun."

The House Party was a rural neighborhood affair with fifteen or twenty people in attendance. People brought food, "a dish to pass," and the musicians were local folks, mostly farmers. The parlor rug was rolled back, the musicians, two or three, played accordion, fiddle and guitar or banjo. The musicians sat in a corner or sometimes in a doorway between the kitchen and the parlor so the music, which was not amplified, could be heard in both rooms. Later in the evening the musicians would take a break and lunch would be served — then more music.

The party could last all night. Party goers would pass the hat and take up a collection for the musicians. The last song of the night was often "Home Sweet Home."

If there was any alcohol at the party, it was usually handled pretty discreetly. Sometimes there might be a jug of homemade wine or some home brew beer in the milk house or behind the shed. My Uncle Lawrence (who played the fiddle) told me he had played a house party with a bandonion (a type of concertina) player by the name of Henry "Step and a Half" Hanson. Henry had a bad leg and limped. After they had played a while, Henry said he was going out for some fresh air. When he came back into the house he had a tell-tale red ring around his mouth which my uncle said came from drinking red wine from a jug.

I remember one party I went to with my parents when I was quite young. The farm had a wind mill generator to furnish the power for their lights, which were rather dim compared to our electric lights today. I remember it as quite cozy. They had a guitar, fiddle and button accordion playing. I remember them dancing a square dance called the Texas Star in which two couples had their arms on each others' shoulders, four people in a group. They swung around in a circle until the ladies' feet flew off the floor. It looked like a lot of fun.

They also played waltzes, polkas, schottisches and two steps. It was a close-knit group of neighbors and relatives, very warm, like a big family gathering. There were people from every age group, all sharing lots of food and conversation. I think this is something we have lost in today's busy life with everybody going their own separate way, doing their own thing. When I hear House Party music, it brings back memories of a simpler time when neighbors got together and visited and had fun.

I would like to thank my mother and her family for the gift of music and for encouraging me to play. Without her help this book would not have been written. I would also like to thank Dix Bruce, my collaborator, for his expertise and technical help. I have to mention some of the old fiddlers and accordion players who played these House Party songs including Herman Erickson, Johnny Homme, Emil Simpson, Roy Anderson, Henry Hanson, Cousin Olin Jacobson, Uncle Windy Whitford, Smokey George Gilbertsen, Art Lewton, Selmer Orin, Carl Winden, Walt Tipton, and many others. And one more big thank you to my wife, Gloria, for her patience and encouragement.

I would like to thank all the old time musicians who passed their music down to the next generation and the next. It is my hope that this collection of songs will help to preserve this music form and pass it on to the next generation. So, let this music carry you back to a time when friends and relatives and neighbors got together and "made their own fun." I hope you will make some of your own.

Bruce Bollerud
June 2004

Bruce Bollerud

Bruce Bollerud was born and raised on a farm in southwestern Wisconsin. His parents were Norwegian-American. Bruce was introduced to music at an early age when he attended house parties in the neighborhood with his family. He began to play the bandonion (a concertina-like instrument) at age 10. Soon he was playing house parties with old time fiddlers from the area. He took piano lessons and played trombone in the high school band. He began to play piano accordion when he was 15. He played with area old time dance bands including, The Rhythm Ramblers, Roger Bright, Verne Meisner, Simpson's Night Hawks, Dick Sherwood and The Goose Island Ramblers. Bruce's earliest musical training and experience was the music or the house party which was largely Norwegian with some of the old pop two steps thrown in. This music was unique in style. Hopefully, this collection will help preserve and promote it.

Bruce Bollerud at the Beehive Pub in Brize-Norton, England while serving in the Air Force 1958

Bruce Bollerud playing the bandonion 1954

Family Reunion 1994 L to R: Ray Brusveen, Bruce, Ed Fitzsimmons, "Cousin Ole" Venden.

Emil Simpson Orch in 1953 Bruce (l) on trombone & bandonian (& piano)

Bruce Bollerud playing with a Swiss group late 1950s
L to R: Herman Feller Jr, Herman Feller Sr, Bobby Feller, Betty Knebuhl, Bruce

Fiddler Herman Erickson & Paul Hughes on banjo.

6

Bruce Bollerud and Norwegian-American Music

The Goose Island Ramblers ca. 1964,
l to r: George Gilbertsen, Wendy Whitford, Bruce Bollerud

The southwestern Wisconsin farming country where Bruce Bollerud was born and raised looks like the picture-postcard stereotype of the rural Midwest. The rolling hills are dominated by hay and corn fields; hardwood forests still cover the steeper hilltops and creekbeds. This landscape is dotted with dairy farmsteads that feature huge barns, usually painted red, flanked by towering silos. Most of the farm houses are about a century old, and white is their most common color. As they prospered, farmers built these houses to replace the modest log structures that the immigrant pioneers to the area originally erected in the mid-1800s.

They had come from Norway, Switzerland, Germany, Bohemia, Ireland, Wales and Cornwall. The immigrants clustered with their co-nationals so each town had and still has a predominant ethnic makeup. Since the arrival of these nineteenth century settlers, the area has not been a magnet for new immigration. The names on the oldest headstones in crossroads cemetaries match those on the RFD mailboxes along the county roads.

Wisconsin people often stress that we have the four seasons, by which we mean that there's a bit of temperate spring and fall between summers that can be very hot and winters that are very cold. And those cold winters can hang on. Before the recent bout of global warming everyone knew snow would cover the ground about Thanksgiving Day and you'd next see the grass in April — about four and a half months later. Those long cold winters have served as a deep freeze for preserving the Old World ethnic music traditions. In the winter you can't work in the fields, so after your milking chores were done there would be time to get together for musical house parties in the rural neighborhood, for old time dances.

Around Bruce's Hollandale home, the Norwegian fiddle and accordion music predominated, but Irish, Germans and Swiss from nearby communities contributed their tunes to the local repertoire and old time American tunes filtered in too. The music Bruce shares in this collection is a heritage of the Old World that slowly evolved in the rural Upper Midwest. The collection is a window into an intimate world. The old time house parties are infrequent now but Bruce has preserved the tunes on these pages. Thank you Bruce for sharing this legacy with us.

Rick March
Wisconsin Arts Board

Goose Island Ramblers 1998

7

The Tunes and Where They Come From

When I interviewed Bruce Bollerud in April 2002, I asked him about the House Party era and also about each of the tunes he collected for this book. Some of my questions and his answers follow.

Dix Bruce

Dix Bruce: Tell us about house party music.

Bruce Bollerud: I lived on a farm in south western Wisconsin, and heard house party music at our house and at neighbors' houses. There were dances on weekend nights in people's homes, rural people playing music. You'd go to the neighbor's farm, they'd roll back the rug in the parlor — they didn't have wall to wall carpeting in those days, they just had a rug — sometimes they'd move the kitchen stove right out of the kitchen! They'd make as much room as they could for dancing. And then, the little band, which would be a two or three piece outfit usually, would set up in a corner and play.

DB: What was the instrumentation of these bands?

BB: They'd always have a guitar for the rhythm, sometimes it could be a banjo, plus a fiddle and an accordion. It'd be some combination of those instruments. Sometimes it might be a guitar and a fiddle, sometimes it might be a guitar and an accordion.

DB: The guitar player probably didn't take leads.

BB: No. He was strictly rhythm. The lead players would play in unison. I don't think they played harmonies that much. Some did, but not that much. Three, four minutes per song, probably, as long as people danced.

DB: How did they mix up the different kinds of tunes?

BB: More waltzes than anything, old time waltzes. And then they would throw in a schottische or two, more waltzes, and then maybe a polka, more waltzes and a two-step. The waltzes were fiddle waltzes with a certain sound from the bow work, three chord songs, most of them, they weren't too complicated. They were rhythmic, they had a certain tempo and a certain swing that the Norwegian waltzes have. They could be Norwegian, Swedish, I don't think so much Danish. There weren't many Danes in the area where I grew up.

DB: Did this music come from a fiddle tradition in the old country?

BB: Absolutely. The accordionists learned from the fiddlers. The fiddle is kind of the national instrument of Scandinavia. The accordion came along a little later in the 1830s, I suppose. They were Hohner two-row button accordions to begin with, the three-row came a little bit later. The accordion has carved out a niche of its own, playing not only the fiddle tunes but also tunes written expressly for the accordion.

DB: In your introduction to this book you said that you came along kind of at the tail end of the house party era.

BB: This would be in the middle to late forties and maybe the early fifties. It was a gradual process, but as the automobile came in and became more common, people began to go farther for a night's entertainment. Before that, they had stayed right in their own little neighborhoods and their own little towns. Once the car came in, they began to travel to the next town, and somebody realized they could put on a dance at a hall and maybe get two, three hundred people to come in, charge them a buck a piece, pay the band, and make some money. So, when that began to happen it was sort of the "in" thing. House parties were local to each little rural community and people began to go the hall dances further away.

DB: Did people pay to go to the house parties?

BB: They usually passed the hat for the band. People bought food and drink. There'd be a lunch served. They were invitational parties, farmers would invite the neighbors and friends and some relatives. You might have twenty or thirty people, maybe, at a big house party. And you knew everybody there. If a stranger walked in, he'd better know somebody. There wasn't going to be any harm come to him, but he'd get the cold shoulder. House parties were fairly temperate, I would say, except that somebody would sometimes have a jug out in the milk house, or behind a tree. It might be home brew, it might be home made wine or whatever. Some of the guys would sneak out and have a sip or two. They were pretty careful not to get too liquored up.

DB: Was it during WWII that you were first exposed to house party music?

BB: Yes. The house parties might have had a slight resurgence around that time because a lot of the musicians were gone to the service.

DB: You started out playing bandonion?

BB: Yes. It's kind of a big concertina. It's a "push-pull" instrument (the same button gives a different note depending upon whether you pull or push, like a harmonica) but it does have a chromatic range. Each note is played on two different buttons. For example, a C here on push, there on pull. I was ten when I started. There was a fellow in the neighborhood who had played bandonion. He'd switched to accordion, but he gave me a few pointers and a sheet or two of music. The music had numbers on it and a symbol for push or pull, so you kind of got the idea of what to do from that. My mother encouraged me to play the bandonion. She had heard bandonion music when she was young and she preferred it to accordion. She said the bandonion had a sweeter sound.

DB: When did you switch to accordion and why?

BB: When I was about thirteen or fourteen, I took piano lessons for two or three years. So I knew the keyboard. And then Frankie Yankovic came through the country in about 1951 or '52, somewhere in there, and was very popular in the old time business. You could play that music on the bandonion, but it didn't have the same sound and it was easier to play on the accordion. You could play more difficult stuff quicker on the accordion. The thing about the bandonion is that you had possibilities, potential there, with the left hand, because you had all single notes, as opposed to pre-set chords on the accordion, which are handy, but limiting. At the time, the accordion was kind of the route to go, and I did. All the big guys, like Yankovic, played piano accordion.

DB: The rock guitar of your day?

BB: Kind of. There was a big accordion craze in the fifties and probably a little earlier, but I didn't take lessons on the accordion. I applied what I learned at piano lessons to the accordion.

DB: Why did the fiddle tradition fade out?

BB: When the hall dances started up, when the Six Fat Dutchmen and Frankie Yankovic and all these guys became popular, the cool thing was to go to those dances. I can remember when I was a young guy, in my teens, still in high school, I'd go to the dances. That's where the girls were, for one thing, and it the music was exciting. You had a ten-piece brass band up there putting out a lot of stuff, and they were good. I think the fiddle music couldn't compete with it on that level at that time, volume-wise, and it wasn't considered cool. For a time during the transition to accordion and brass band, there were bands that had a fiddle. They would have drums and trumpet or sax, some combination of horns. But these eventually faded out.

DB: Are the keys that you play these tunes in the original fiddle keys?

BB: Mostly. Fiddlers like sharp keys (G, A, D) etc. Part of that is the sound they get with those open strings on the fiddle and they ring more.

DB: When you play these songs you seem the have a specific idea of what tempo to play each tune at. How did you develop that? Where does it come from?

BB: I don't know, you just kind of feel it. It's like if somebody would ask you, "How do you know when to change chord from D to G?" or whatever it might be. How do you actually know that? I couldn't tell you how I actually "know" that. I know it's going to happen, I know I have to go to G next. I can't give you a rule for the tempos.

DB: It must go back to playing for dancers.

BB: Within certain parameters. There's a certain feeling. Like with a Viennese waltz, kind of a majestic feeling almost. The Norwegian waltzes have kind of an earthiness to them.

DB: Before you mentioned the term "swing."

BB: They (Norwegian waltzes) do, of course all music swings if it's good. If you play it the right tempo and you play it right, it all swings.

DB: How did you learn these songs? By repetition with the fiddlers you played with?

BB: Mostly, yes. I think music is made up of a lot of clichés and a particular style will have particular little clichés that tend to happen again and again. You can kind of string them together, or at least that's the way I've organized it. The first thing I usually do if I'm learning a piece is to get the chord progression down so I know where it's going to change. And then I start picking out the melody.

DB: You learned a lot of these songs from a man you played with for many years in the Goose Island Ramblers, Wendy Whitford. Could you talk a little bit about how Wendy learned them and how he passed them on to you?

BB: I'm sure that he played along with some of these old fiddlers that were old when he was young (in the 1920s and 1930s). He mentions Ryerson, Ole Gutrud, and George Matson, a whole bunch of people that I never knew but heard about forever. They were probably playing at a house party and he probably sat down beside them, watched their fingers and listened. He did a remarkable job. He wasn't a Norwegian, but when he played those Norwegian pieces, he was Norwegian in his heart. He really felt that music.

DB: Talk about the individual tunes.

BB: **Kjarring Og Mann Slust** or "The Old Man and his Wife Fighting." That's a song I learned from Everett Kittleson and he learned it from Orville Runehaug and I don't know where Orville got it from. It's a two part song, and the way Everett explained it me is that the first part is calm and easy going. That's the man. The second part is a little more chattery and that's the woman. It's kind of a little joke! At least the men laugh when they hear that explanation.

Sally's Hoppwaltz Polka. "Sally" is actually Selmer Oren but they called him Sally as a nickname, and he was an old time fiddler. He had a lot of good pieces and that was one that he played. I didn't learn it from him though, I learned it from Art Leuten from Stoughton, (WI) who had learned it from him, and it's just a real good hoppwaltz. A hoppwaltz is not a waltz, it's a polka. They dance it with like a Polish hop, and the Norwegians have always called that a "hoppwaltz." Whoever named it must have seen some similarity with the steps of the waltz, somehow, but it isn't a waltz. The hoppwaltz has a step pattern that goes, "1—2—3" then a hop. That could explain the term "hoppwaltz " since the waltz also goes "1—2—3." And, "Sally's Hoppwaltz Polka" is not in 3/4 time, it's a polka.

The Stegen Waltz means "The Step Ladder Waltz." The first part is basically the same tune as "Tobacco Setter's Waltz," with just a little alteration. Don't you think that's kind of odd to name a waltz after a step ladder?

Red Rooster Two Step. Wendy Whitford played that for George (Gilbertsen) and I when we recorded in 1999 and we said, "When did you learn that Wendy?" He said, "Aw, I played that fifty years ago," or whatever it was. We said, "Well, you never played it for us." He said, "I guess I didn't." We said, "How come?" He said, "Well I guess I didn't think of it!" There was a song that he'd had for years. We'd played together for thirty five years (as the Goose Island Ramblers) and never heard that song. No telling how many other songs he might have had. "Red Rooster" is a ragtime piece and it's interesting that the second part is in a minor key. It's neat that string band musicians listened to ragtime music, which was popular in the day. I wonder how the title came about.

Skjorte Frak Waltz is the "Shirt Tail Waltz." I don't know the significance of that. I kind of see in my mind's eye somebody dancing all night long and maybe a guy's shirt came out, or something like that, kind of flopping around as he was dancing.

Herman's Schottische in D I learned from Herman Erickson, who was the first fiddle player that I played with. I didn't know it at the time, but later on I heard George Gilbertsen played a similar tune "Flop Eared Mule," which he calls "The Big Eared Mule." A lot of people play "Flop Eared Mule" as a hoe-down tune. Herman played it as a schottische, and I've heard some other Norwegians play it that way. I suspect they heard this hoe-down tune, slowed it down, and turned it into a schottische. And it works very well. Herman was a big influence on me. We would go to his house and practice and then find places to play…amateur contests, house parties, tavern jobs, etc. He usually drove and my mother and dad went with too. It was hard to quit playing with Herman when I started playing in a dance band. I've always felt some regret about that. I think Herman felt kind of bad.

Gra Lysining means "the gray light of morning." I learned that from Herman Erickson too. These house parties would last all night long, and people would be walking or driving home in the *gra lysining*. Getting light, but the sun isn't up yet.

DB: There are several songs here that mention Ryerson. Who was Ryerson?

11

BB: He was an old fiddler, I think it was Clarence Ryerson, who Wendy Whitford used to listen to when Wendy was young. He must have been a crackerjack because all of his pieces are good. They're nice, solid pieces. I really would have liked to have heard him when he was in his prime.

DB: Was **Ryerson's Hoppwaltz** the name that Ryerson had for the song?

BB: I doubt it very much. These guys didn't name pieces after themselves very often. He probably called it something else, might have been "Olson's Waltz" or whatever. Wendy knew it as "Ryerson's."

Auction Pa Strommen. Wendy told me they had an auction at Strommen's. Strommen is a Norwegian name, and they went down there for the auction and it rained that day. So, the auction kind of fizzled out and they went in the house and had a house party. They played the fiddle. I'm not sure who was playing the fiddle, if it was Ryerson or one of those old guys that Wendy talked about, but that was one of the pieces and Wendy learned it. That's an unusual piece because the first part is in C and the second part goes to D. That's kind of an unusual change. Usually you'd go from C to G or C to F, but C, right into D is unusual. It's kind of neat though because the second half of the second part goes up to G temporarily and then back down to D. And then, when you go back to C, you just drop down from D to C. Unusual for an old time tune.

Minnesota Six Eight Two Step. I met this fiddle band, two fiddles, a banjo, and a guitar, from Mabel, Minnesota. Erik Bye, a big television producer and star in Norway, had come over here to America to tape programs of Norwegian American musicians, artists, and craftspeople for Norwegian television. He called me and asked me to come up to Minneapolis and play on this show. I thought that was kind of neat because they got to see me in Norway. While I was up there, I met these old fellows who were playing these tunes and they gave me a tape of their stuff. "Minnesota Six Eight Two Step" was learned from them.

Johnny Homme's Waltz. Johnny Homme was a neighbor of ours from Hollandale, lived about a mile and a half away. He was an old fiddler and we played a few house parties together and that was one that he played. I'm real sorry that I didn't record more of his stuff. Most of the old fiddler's were a little rough, their technique wasn't real tight, but he was very smooth and accurate in what he did. I'm sure I lost a lot of good pieces there that I didn't get, and he's dead now, so they're gone.

Sentimental Selma. There was a big Scandinavian dialect humor thing going on from the teens (1911-1919), and up, and they did songs either in Norwegian or Swedish, and they also did them in English with a comic Scandinavian accent, and this was one of those. My mother's name was Selma, so I always think of her whenever I play it. In the song, Sentimental Selma "went to Hollywood to act like Greta Garbo," who was a Swede, of course. "Barnum said she could." Then it goes, "I think you are the cutest girl I ever knew, your sunny smile thrills me through and through. Yeah, well, Selma you don't have to tell me, your eyes and your smile, *yust* like yesterday." I imagine in my mind that she went out there to Hollywood to try to make it big and maybe she didn't quite make it, maybe she came back sometime later, and maybe this guy is still carrying the torch for her. English lyrics set to a traditional tune.
It was a schottische. The melody had been around a long time. And there are Norwegian lyrics. I've heard several different sets of lyrics in Norwegian. (In Norwegian) *Huk si du en dagen/Jeg møte deg på isen/Da du drogge/den gra stygge griesen.* That means, "Do you remember the day I met you one the ice? When you were dragging the old gray pig."

Art's Waltz is from Art Lewton of Stoughton, Wis. I think he got it from a man by the name of Andrew Kleven. That's as much as he knew about it. He had heard this other fiddler play it and he learned it. These tunes are really handed from one musician to the next. I'm sure somebody "wrote" them at some point back, but it might be a long time ago. You might be looking at a hundred years ago.

Almando's Polka. Almando was one of the guys from the Mabel, Minnesota, fiddle band, I can't remember his last name, but I had talked mostly with him and he gave me most of these things.

Abner Juve's Waltz. Abner Juve was another man I didn't know, but somebody that Wendy had heard when he was young and Wendy played a few of his songs.

Mabel's Rag Two Step and **Mabel Polka** and two more tunes from the Mabel, Minnesota, fiddle band.

Ryerson's Waltz. Another tune learned from Wendy Whitford, who learned it from Clarence Ryerson.

Art's Schottische. Another tune learned from Art Lewton of Stoughton, Wis.

Grandpa's Waltz. I'm not sure, but the "grandpa" referred to in the titles could be Wendy Whitford's grandfather. Same with **Grandpa's Mazurka.** I kind of doubt that Wendy's grandpa would have written either. He probably just liked those tunes and Wendy named them according to that.

Sugar Candy Schottische. *(In Norwegian: "Sukkertoy")* I got this song from an accordion player from Hollandale, (Wis.), Gilbert Prestebroten. He had some real good old time pieces and that was one of them. I had played in his band when I was sixteen years old. I had been playing with the old fiddlers, at house parties and things. Gilbert had a band before the war and during the war they kind of broke it up because most of the guys were drafted. After the war, probably in the early fifties, he decided to start a band again. He came over to our farm and I was milking a cow, and he started talking to me. And, like Norwegians do, he talked about the weather and he talked about the crops, and he talked about this and that. Finally, he asked if I would like to play with his band. I was real excited about that, I was sixteen at the time and now I was going to go play with one of those dance hall bands. I played piano and trombone, but mostly piano with the Rhythm Ramblers. Gilbert played accordion. It was an old time dance band: polkas and waltzes and fox trots. They didn't call them "polka" bands in those days, they called them "old time" bands as opposed to "modern" bands which played "Star Dust," "In the Mood," and things like that.

Old Utica Waltz is one that Wendy Whitford played and he learned it from one of those old fiddlers, I don't know who. He thought the name of it was the "Old Utica Waltz." It may or may not be the "Old Utica Waltz," but that's what he called it.

Johnny's Swiss Polka is from Johnny Mueller. He played the bandonion. When I was twelve, thirteen years old, playing the bandonion, all the bandonion players knew each other, it seemed like. There were bandonion players from Durand, Ill, that would come up, Freddie Elmer, and Johnny Mueller from Darlington, (Wis.), and Johnny Schneider from New Glarus, (Wis.), a Mr. Legler from Dodgeville, (Wis.). All these bandonion players would go around and listen to each other. It was kind of like a little club, almost, and that was nice. That was the piece that Johnny played. He had given me the music to it except that it wasn't written out in notes. He used a number system that had a series of dots to indicate how long a note should be held.

The Tobacco Setter's Waltz. When they plant the tobacco, the tobacco setters had to ride on a little rig and set the tobacco plant in the ground, each one individually. Obviously that piece had to have come from around Stoughton or Edgerton (Wis.), somewhere in that area where they raised tobacco. This tune is similar to "The Stegen Waltz."

13

Johnson's Rhinelander Schottische. There's no specific "Johnson," it's kind of a generic title. I had that song on tape and Gilbert Prestebroten announced the name of it but I can't make it out because somebody coughed or something just as he said it. It was something like "Johnson," not really Johnson, but I just tacked it on. You gotta have *something* on there! The "Rhinelander" is a style of schottische. The influence came from Germany, I'm sure.

Cousin Olin's Waltz. Cousin Olin was a first cousin to my mother up in New Auburn, Wis., and he played the three-row button accordion. He learned that waltz from a traveling salesman that came through selling something. Whatever it was he sold, this guy would come into town and play the accordion a little bit to get people in the mood and then present his sales pitch. It's an unusual waltz with a kind of a Hawaiian effect to it. I wonder if it was influenced by the Hawaiian music that was popular in the early part of the century. Maybe Hawaiian music drifted into the house party group too.

Ole's Schottische. "Ole" is just a generic Norwegian in this particular case. There's another name on the tape that I learned the tune from, but I don't know what it is, and I had to name it something. So I named it "Ole's Schottische" for all the Oles out there.

DB: It's the classic folk process: as a new person hears and performs an old tune, the melody or harmony might be changed a little bit, and, as you've said, the titles got changed and re-arranged.

BB: Yes, they did.

DB: Most of the tunes in this set are in major keys.

BB: Most of the Norwegian or Scandinavian pieces in this country were in a major key. In the old country, they used minor keys a lot. The major key was still the predominant key but they used minors a good deal. Norwegian-American fiddle tunes are a whole different art form than the tunes played in Norway. They're related, obviously, but they're different. I think they're simpler, tend to be in the major key, tend to be two part songs, as opposed to three part songs (in the old country). Norwegian-American fiddlers simplified the tunes. I think they did that because they were not professional musicians. They were farmers, working people. Those old farmers had big, strong hands that probably didn't move as quick a professional musician's hands would, so they did what they could do.

DB: Why do you think the Scandinavian Americans left the minor keys largely behind?

BB: First of all, the weather, the sun doesn't shine as much over there. It's cloudier and rainier, that kind of dampens your spirits a little bit sometimes. At the time of the immigrants, back in the 1850s and before, people were oppressed, they were poor, back in Norway. There wasn't much hope for advancement. You couldn't marry a rich man's daughter, you stayed in your own class. When they got over here, things opened up, there was hope. If you worked hard, and if you were fairly smart with how you did things, you could make some money. I think major keys are happier than minor keys. Also they may have felt they had more personal and artistic freedom in the new country. They didn't have to follow a form that was already established, they could do their own. They didn't have to tip their hat to some minister or official of the government that came by. And, they heard other kinds of music. They heard American music and English music, and Irish music and German music, and they took bits and pieces from all of this and strained it through their own experience and came up with new things.

DB: What do you think the future is for these kinds of tunes?

BB: Well, it's kind of bleak, I'm afraid. The old fiddlers that play these tunes are dying off. Some of the tunes are being picked up, but not very many, and most of them haven't been written down, that I know of. There's a fairly good body of these that are recorded. I know that Jim Leary, Rick March, Phil Martin and some other people have recorded musicians playing some of these things. Also LeRoy Larsen of Minneapolis and Bob Andreason of Duluth (now deceased) have collected a lot of Norwegian-American music. So, there are some things that are taped and they won't be lost totally in that regard. The only thing is, unless these pieces get out where the public can hear them, and unless some younger musician take them up, they become museum pieces. That's better than nothing, because someone can always go back and pull them out, but I don't know that they will.

I think one of the things that happened here is that folk music has been popularly thought of as coming out of the South and the West, but you don't hear people talk a lot about folk music coming from the Midwest. I'm not sure why that is. Consequently, the researchers and the people like Alan Lomax and all these people who went back and recorded these obscure little tunes in the hills, didn't come up here and do that very much. So, some of that stuff has just withered on the vine.

DB: It seems that there was a certain group of folklorists who were most interested in cultures that were most different from their own traditions. I guess we needed to have folklorists from the South looking at the North and saying, "Gee, how interesting." It may also be that in the early part of the century, since the Civil War or even before, there was so much romanticizing of the South in popular culture, the plantation, the happy workers, and that, that anything from the South was thought of as exotic. Like Hawaiian music later on or periods when Japanese or Chinese things were thought to be especially interesting or romantic. I don't know of anyone of the stature of a Lomax or a Seeger looking at this culture from the outside and chronicling it the way other cultures have been recorded and collected.

BB: I don't know why they didn't look at this culture, but they didn't, apparently. It's funny. Polkas are a folk music, certainly, what else could you call them? But people who follow folk music seem to kind of look down on polkas. They don't regard it as a folk music. Maybe because after the house party era, polka or "old time" music was played by professional bands like Whoopie John, the Six Fat Dutchmen, and Frankie Yankovic.

DB: Do you think this Scandinavian music could find an audience outside of that ethnic community?

BB: Absolutely! I could see a bluegrass group playing this stuff like nothing! It would fit. It's in the right key and being fiddle driven, it has the right nuances.

DB: Most of this music is dance oriented. Probably what we need to do is keep people dancing and they'll continue to want this music.

BB: Of course, people don't dance the way they used to. Even the bluegrass is now a concert type of music. I suspect that they may have danced it earlier on because I don't think the tempos were quite as fast in the beginning, kind of pre-Monroe. This stuff could be jazzed up if you wanted to do it faster (for listening).

DB: What's the best thing that could happen with this music?

BB: I'd like to see younger musicians come in, take up this music and play it. I think of Bluegrass, for example, which has been revived and carried forward by younger musicians. Musicians of national stature, like Rick Skaggs, have come in and given it a great big boost. I don't know that that would happen here, but it would be nice. At least it would be nice if local younger musicians would play some of it before it's gone like a puff of smoke.

Kjarring Og Mann Slust
The Old Man and his Wife Fighting

Musette switch

Arr. by Bruce Bollerud

Sally's Hoppwaltz

Polka

Musette switch

Arr. by Bruce Bollerud

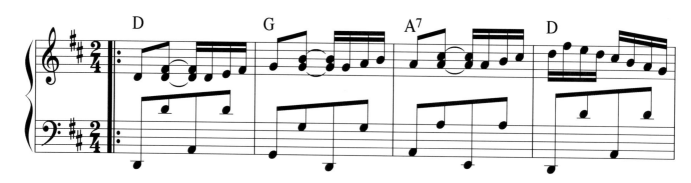

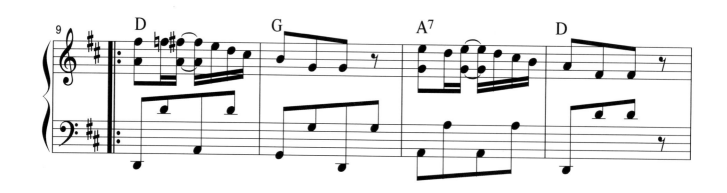

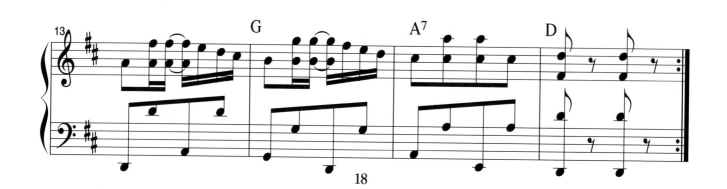

Stegen Waltz

Musette switch

Step Ladder Waltz

Arr. by Bruce Bollerud

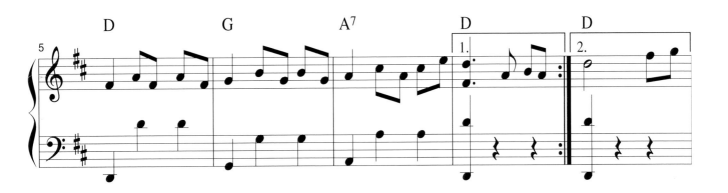

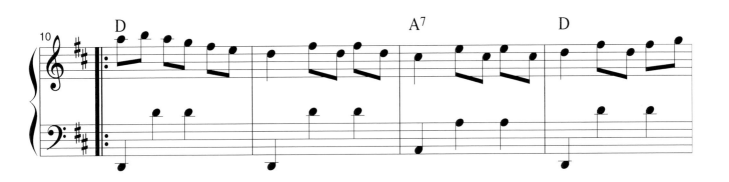

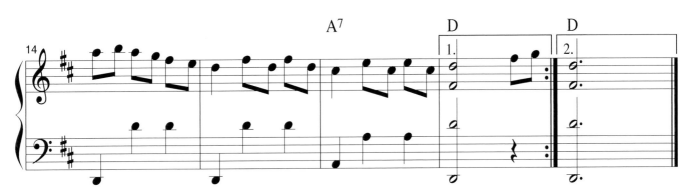

19

Red Rooster Two Step

Arr. by Bruce Bollerud

Skjorte Frak Waltz
Shirt Tail Waltz

Musette switch

Arr. by Bruce Bollerud

23

Herman's Schottische in D

Arr. by Bruce Bollerud

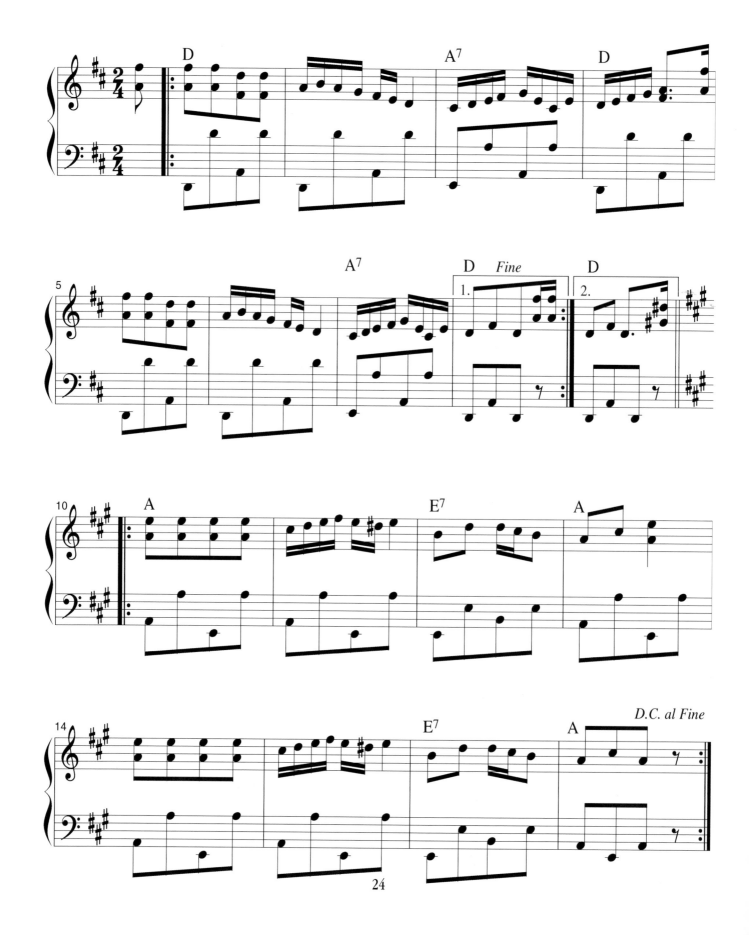

Ryerson's Hoppwaltz

Polka

Arr. by Bruce Bollerud

Musette switch

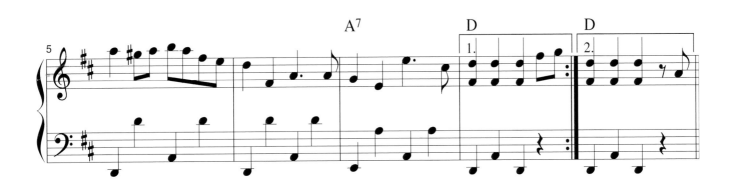

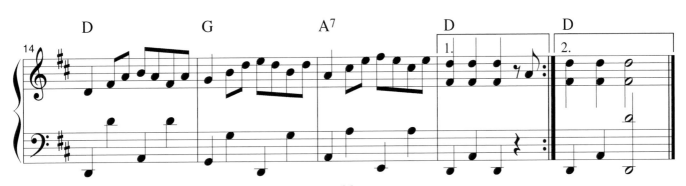

25

Gra Lysining

In the Gray Light of the Morning

Arr. by Bruce Bollerud

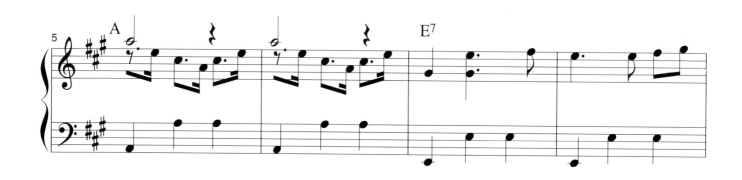

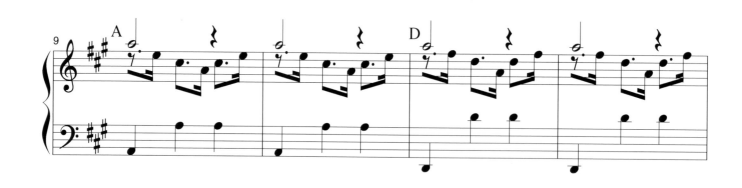

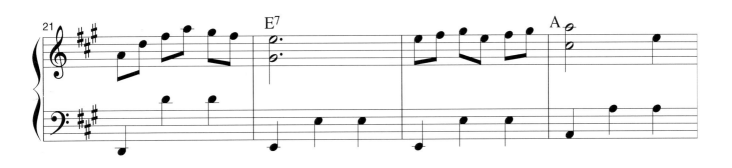

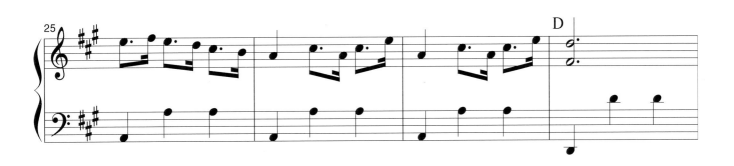

27

Auction Pa Strommen

The Auction at Strommen's

Musette switch

Arr. by Bruce Bollerud

28

Johnny Homme's Waltz

Arr. by Bruce Bollerud

Musette switch

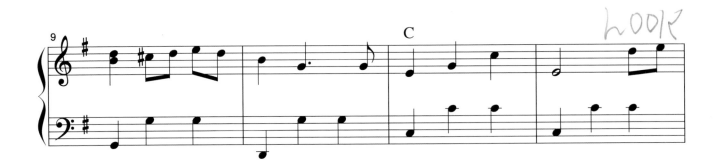

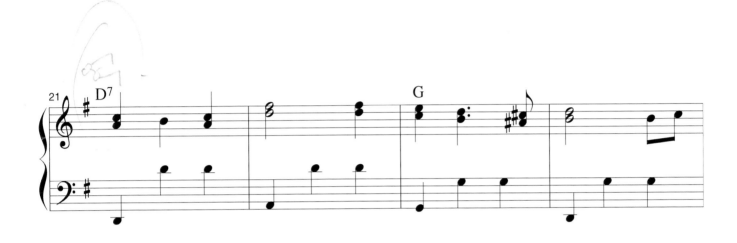

Minnesota 6/8 Two Step

Arr. by Bruce Bollerud

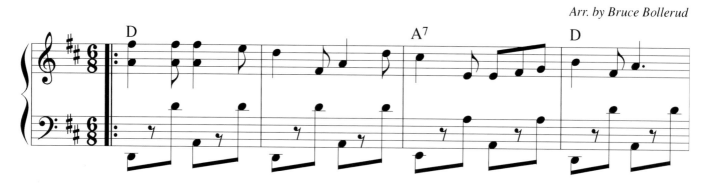

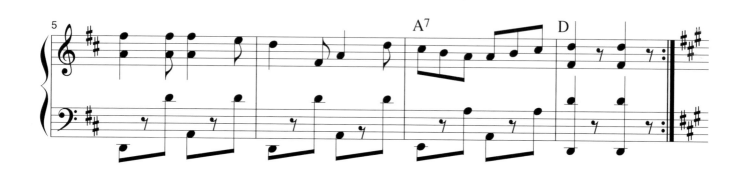

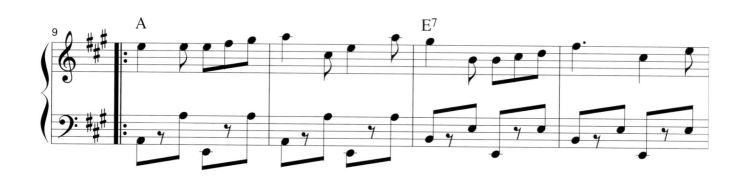

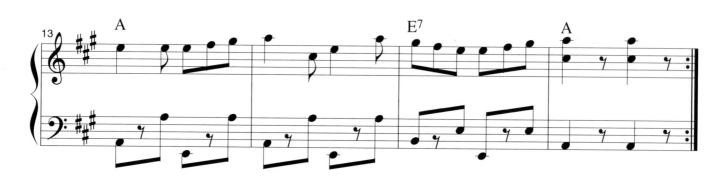

Sentimental Selma

Schottische

Arr. by Bruce Bollerud

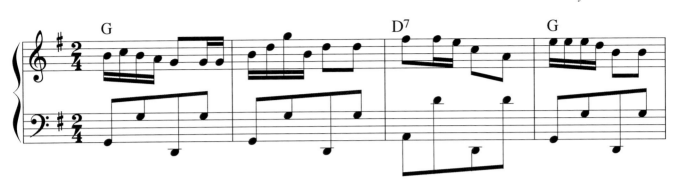

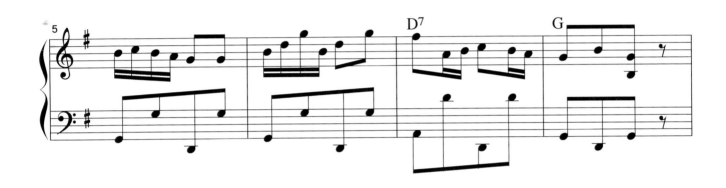

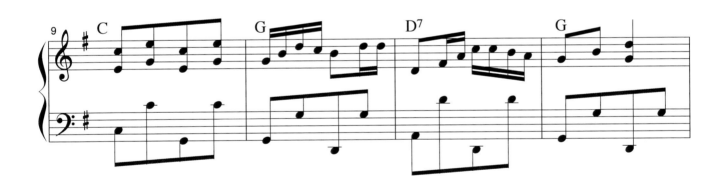

Art's Waltz in A

Arr. by Bruce Bollerud

Almando's Polka

Arr. by Bruce Bollerud

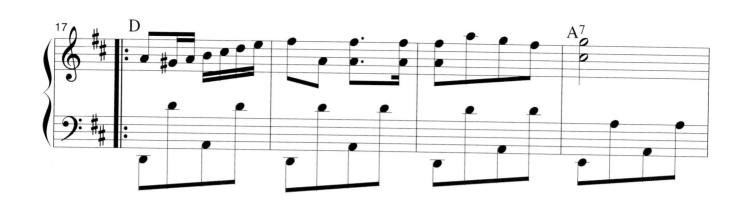

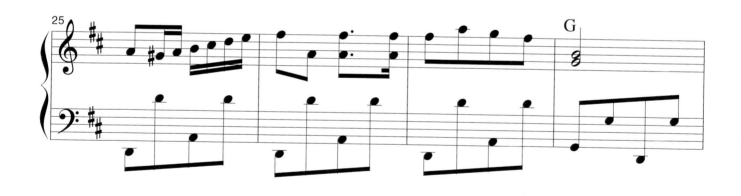

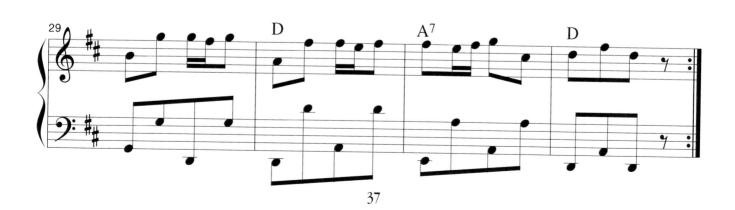

Abner Juve's Waltz

Arr. by Bruce Bollerud

Mabel Rag Two Step

Arr. by Bruce Bollerud

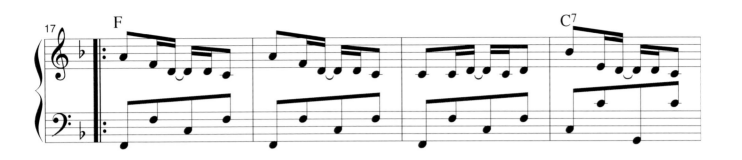

Ryerson's Waltz

Arr. by Bruce Bollerud

Art's Schottische

Musette switch

Arr. by Bruce Bollerud

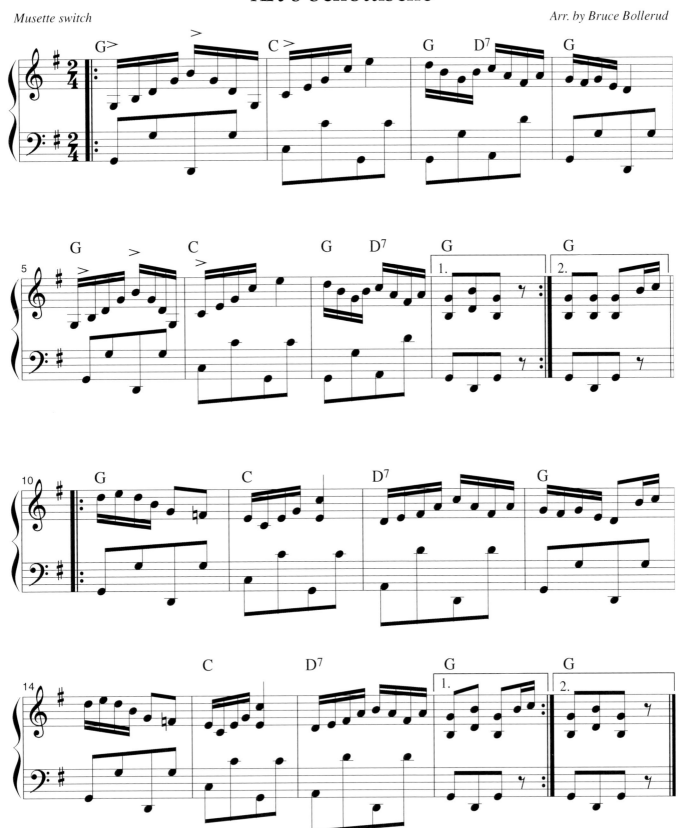

43

Grandpa's Waltz

Arr. by Bruce Bollerud

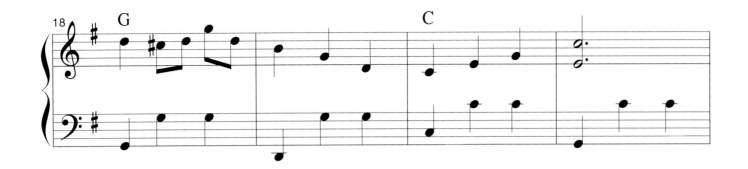

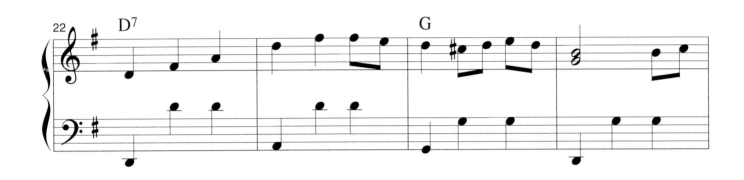

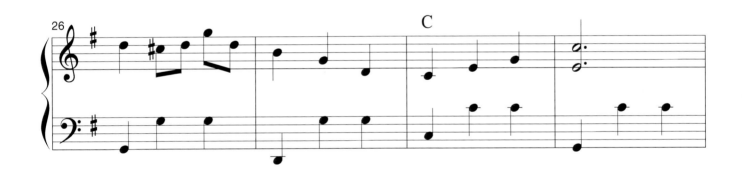

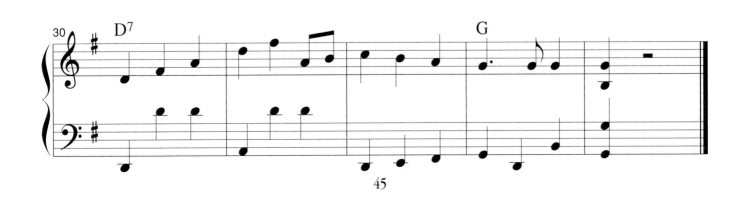

Mabel's Polka

Arr. by Bruce Bollerud

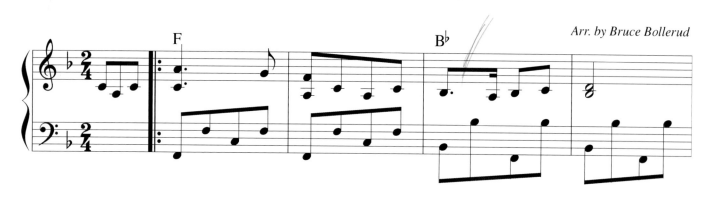

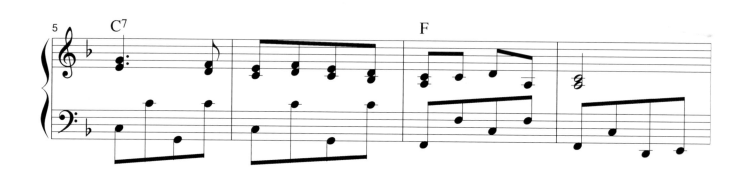

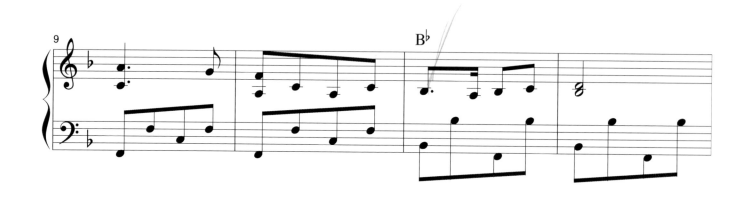

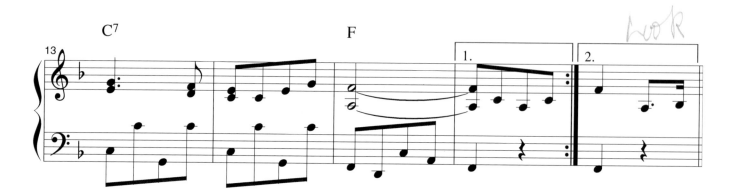

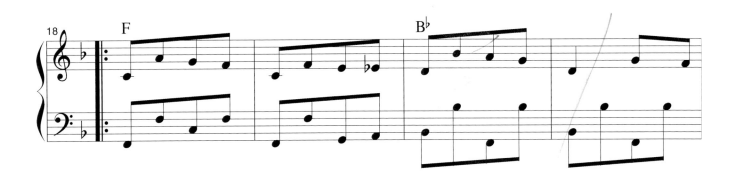

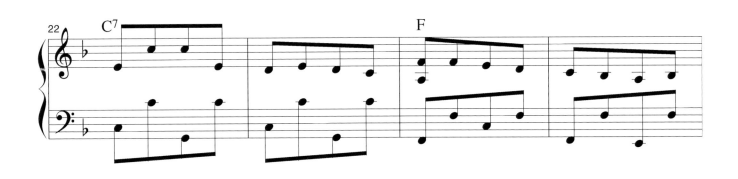

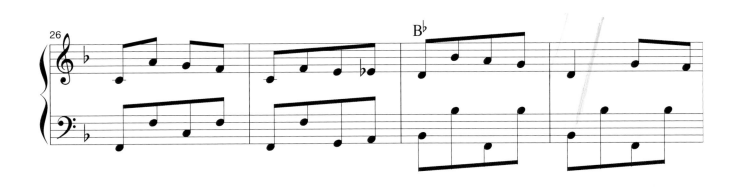

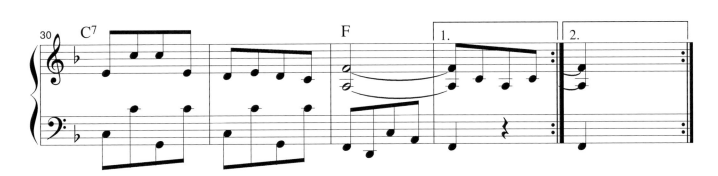

Grandpa's Mazurka

Arr. by Bruce Bollerud

Sugar Candy Schottische

Arr. by Bruce Bollerud

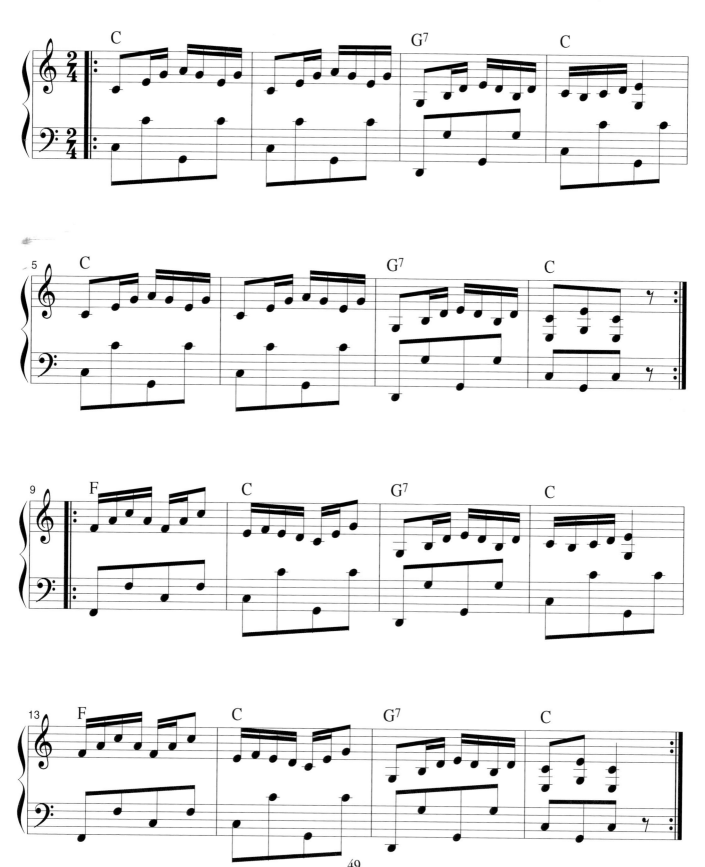

Old Utica Waltz

Arr. by Bruce Bollerud

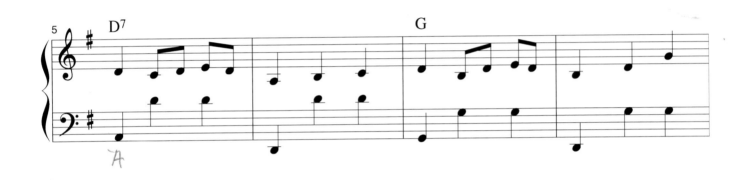

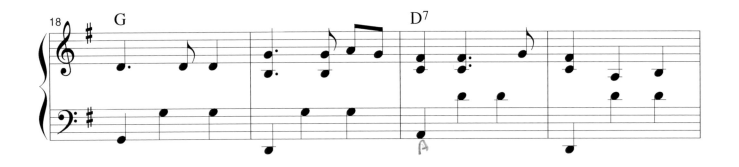

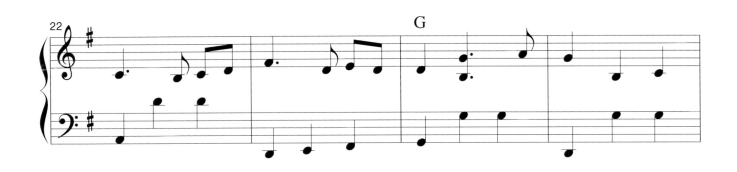

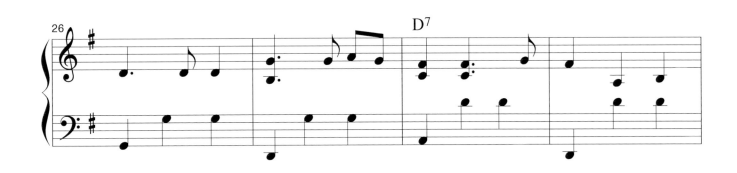

51

Johnny's Swiss Polka

Arr. by Bruce Bollerud

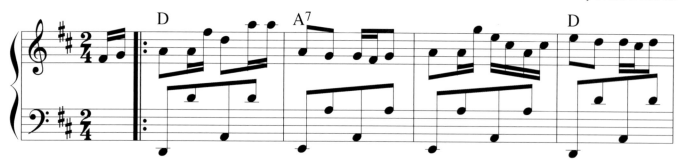

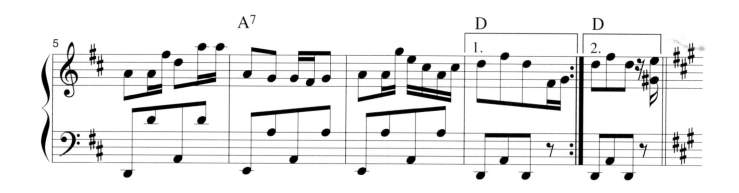

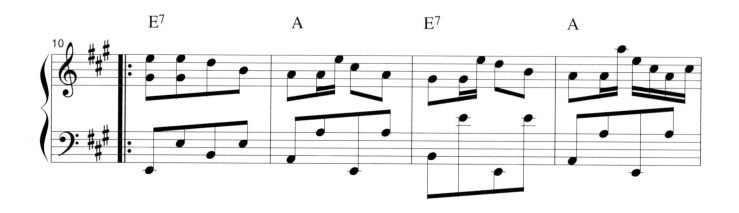

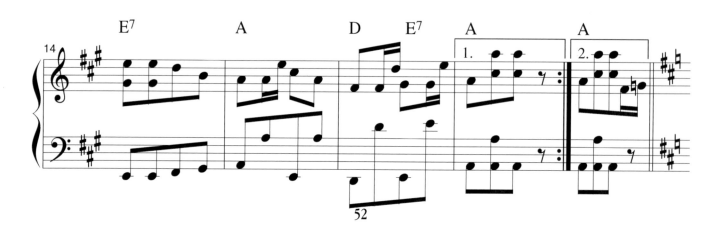

52

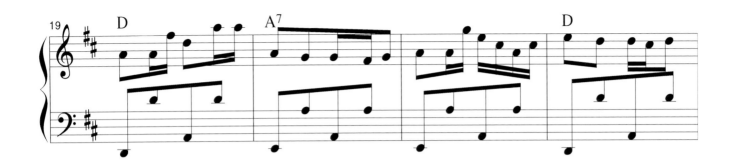

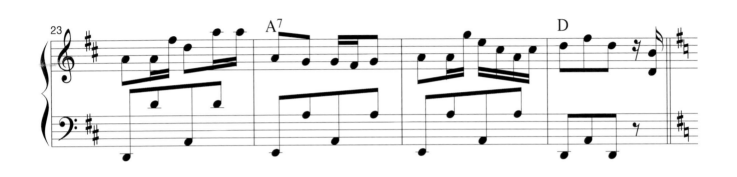

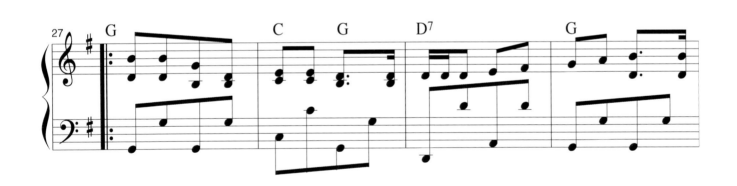

Johnson's Rhinelander Schottische

Arr. by Bruce Bollerud

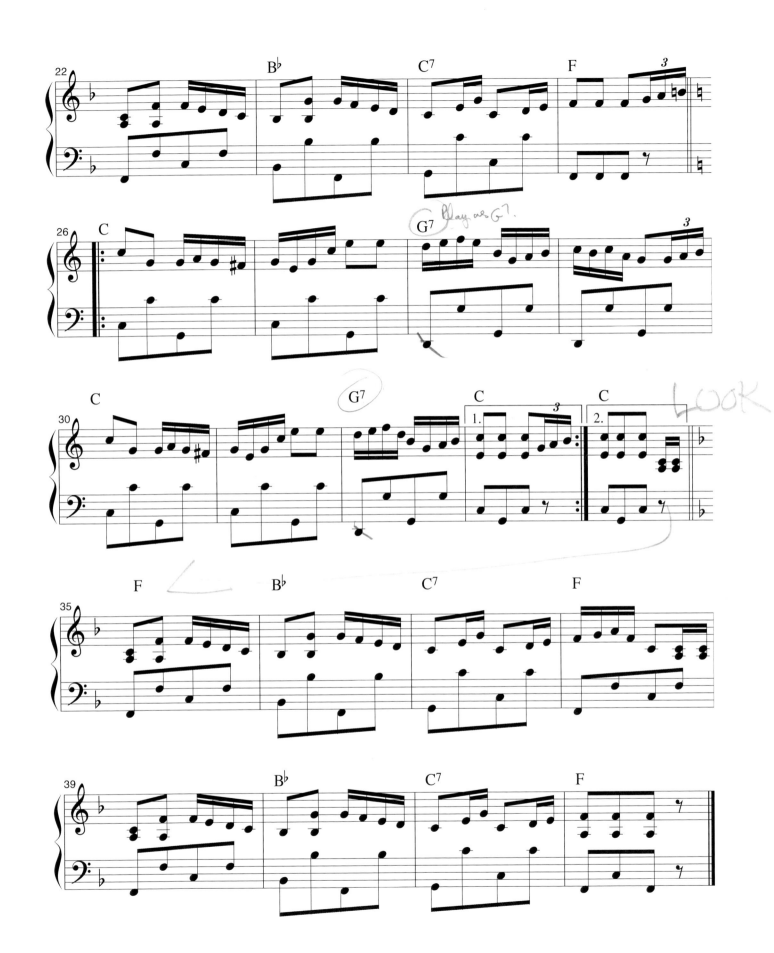

Cousin Olin's Waltz

Musette switch

Arr. by Bruce Bollerud

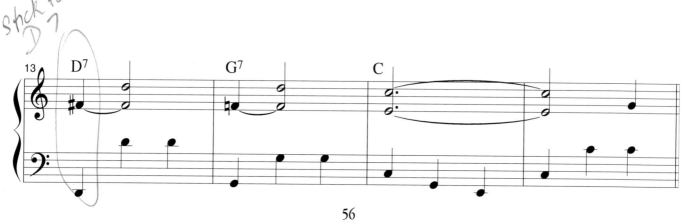

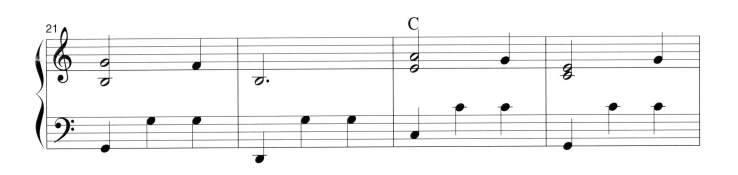

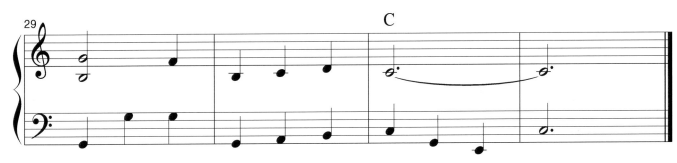

Tobacco Setter's Waltz

Arr. by Bruce Bollerud

Ole's Schottische

Arr. by Bruce Bollerud

Musette switch

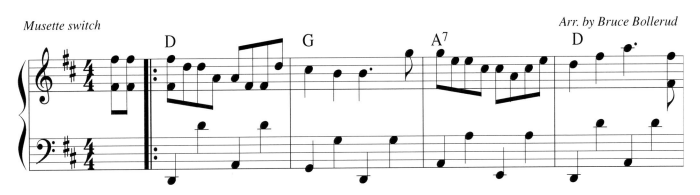

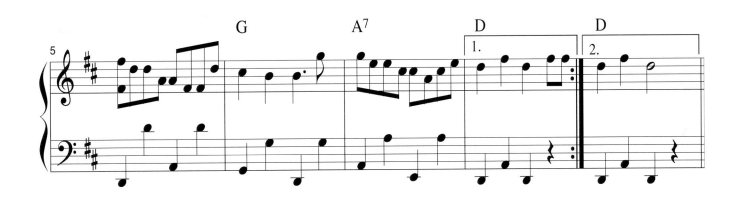

Index